The Reality of Your Enlightenment

How to enter the source of divine bliss inside

by Stephan Wilmes

Copyright © 2022 by Stephan Wilmes

All rights reserved. No part of this book may be reproduced or used in any manner without the written permission of the copyright owner except for the use of quotations in a book review. For more information, address:

info@youinfocusproducts.com
www.goneintogod.com

FIRST EDITION

ISBN: 978-1-7774707-6-0

Acknowledgments

I would like to express my gratitude to the mystical forces of the universe for guiding me through dark and challenging times in my life. Sadness, depression, frustration, anger, pain, and hatred were once my constant companions. Over the years, they have transformed in my perception from adversaries into transcendent companions on the journey of my humanity. Although it may be difficult to comprehend with our conditioned minds, I have come to understand that nothing within us needs to change when we fully embrace, love, and enter the highest reaches of our consciousness—the reality of receiving enlightenment.

When contemplating the vastness and eternity of the universe, with an estimated 200+ billion galaxies, each containing thousands of solar systems like our own, it becomes evident that the creator of our universe has ample space and time. Profound life lessons may take time to integrate fully. It took me the experience of three religious communities/cults to learn the invaluable lesson of never projecting love, wisdom, and light onto others in my life again. I realized that the source of love and happiness can only be found within.

I am profoundly grateful for these powerful and painful lessons, and I am eager to share my discoveries from 30 years of intensive research with you.

With infinite and eternal love, Stephan

Contents

What is Receiving Enlightenment?...8
Neuroscience: Our Brain Creates the Story of Our Life............11
Quantum Physics: Enlightenment is just a glimpse away 16
The Stars are Calling Us Home 20
The Reality of Enlightenment and the Kingdom of God.....22
The Reality of Receiving God/Love/Bliss..................................27
The Projection Game 31
We Are The Miracle 34
The Human Experience And the Divine Experience..................37
Self Acceptance 44
Our Mind, The Golden Retriever..47
Transformation and Transcendence..51
The Purpose of Our Life and the Idea of the Ideal 53
Complete Love..56
The Door To Our Paradise..58
Transcendental Bliss 62
The Function of a True "Spiritual Master" 64
Kill the Buddha 70
Black vs. White Magic..72
Spiritual Groups 75
Reflections Concerning Partnership and Sexuality....................77
You Are The Light of the World 80
Ask And You Will Receive 83
You are the Master..85

What is Breathing your Body?..87
Real Joy...88
Your Book of Love 89
Spiritual Practice 93

Introduction

"We human beings are like most beautiful mighty eagles who choose to stay in their tiny cage because of fear of flying instead of loving the blissful joy of soaring freely in the skies."

I grew up as a child of this world, where the unconditional flow of love and light is regrettably not an integral part of the configuration on this planet. While my parents did their best, their lives were heavily influenced by status, dry religion, and the material world. They, too, learned these values from their parents, and this cycle continued through generations.

As a child and teenager, I often felt sadness and trauma, yearning for nourishment and love. Although I experienced occasional glimpses of genuine love within, my true inner journey began at the age of 30 when I discovered the possibility of experiencing life in the flow of unconditional divine love within.

It's crucial to emphasize that we all share a common human experience. Myself may be marred by flaws and harrowing experiences on the human level, but the profound revelation of my journey is that none of these imperfections matter at all.

Despite a traumatized self, we have the capacity to adore, love, embrace, and revel in the divine experience—the "bliss, light, and love of the kingdom of God." This book aims to illuminate this very path.

For a significant portion of my life, much like many others, the term "enlightenment" appeared as an enigmatic concept. I struggled to relate to it. Instead, I spent my life yearning for love projected onto the external world, particularly the female form, while spiritual enlightenment remained an elusive concept. This book extends an invitation for us to explore the possibility of enlightenment in our lives. As strange and distant as it may initially sound, the words "light" and "love" are always closer to our hearts and minds than we often realize. Scientifically, we all possess a spiritual center in our brains known as the Parietal Cortex. Modern neurological research confirms that we create the "movie" of our lives in our minds. Despite external influences, we all harbor the unlimited potential and power to craft the experiences within our inner world.

Crucially, we need not become perfect love before entering perfect love inside. This realization is pivotal. There's no requirement for perfection in our selves or bodies. We can transition between energy levels, much like atomic particles existing simultaneously in different places and energy states. This is the divine power we hold.

Whatever resonates with you in this book, I encourage you to open up to it and allow its meaning to guide you into the realm of unconditional love.

Chapter 1

What is Receiving Enlightenment?

Enlightenment is simply the realization that eternal, infinite, and unconditional love and light is the origin, essence, and destination of our entire existence.

Enlightenment entails entering this core and ceasing to judge and criticize ourselves for our perfect imperfections.

Enlightenment is lovingly committing to the core of love/light within, where the status of our self becomes completely irrelevant.

The pursuit, approach, and attainment of enlightenment constitute the sole purpose of our human existence.

Buddha ardently recommends enlightenment.

Jesus and Christian mystics refer to enlightenment as the "kingdom of God."

Sufism dances in ecstatic bliss.

Hinduism extols the "bliss of existence."

We perpetually shape our reality through belief and vibration. The term "depression" both reflects and creates a frequency, just as "enlightenment" mirrors and creates a frequency. Both are perceived and constructed within our system.

We heal our traumatized selves with love, which is a energetic and vibrational force. We can also immerse ourselves in the potential of enlightenment by aligning with love and light. This vibration is ever-present, and we simply can allow ourselves to open into it.

This is one of the possibilities available to us as humans: to ascend into a flow of ecstatic, transcendental, and blissful love.

Ecstasy involves transcending our old, limited, and earthbound selves, while transcendence means ascending to a higher, untouchable state of consciousness. Transformation involves a profound and dramatic change in form or appearance.

The "land of a thousand suns" always awaits us in our Parietal Cortex, the spiritual epicenter of our brains. It's the realm of "Wonne," the sensation of supreme joy and bliss. The source of complete and all-encompassing happiness resides within.

We share this love unconditionally, much like new mothers caring for their newborns with tender, loving eyes. We share this love and wisdom without expecting anything in return.

Do not heed confused or manipulative concepts telling you otherwise. This is the most profound form of love that humanity can experience.

Simply close your eyes and turn your senses inward.

It's a state of non-doing.

My practical advice: If your brain and body trouble you, try listening to nature sounds, such as ocean waves, with headphones. Over time, this can help heal your trauma. If you experience significant trauma, have the courage to seek professional therapeutic help, such as IFS-informed EMDR therapy, which my wife Alice specializes in and has greatly benefited her clients.

Chapter 2

Neuroscience: Our Brain Creates the Story of Our Life

Everything in our lives may be different from what we've believed. What I'm sharing may seem scientific and distant, but it has the potential to awaken us to the possibility of enlightenment, manifested as bliss and divine love.

The Old View: Living from the Outside In... In school, we learned that we perceive the physical world through our bodies, using our five basic senses: sight, hearing, smell, taste, and touch. These senses create a perception of separation between us and the external world. We perceive ourselves as "I" (my body, my form) and others as "other people" (other bodies, other forms). For many, the brain is the center of personality and ego, and survival is the predominant focus. "Survival of the fittest" is driven by fear and stress, governing much of our existence.

The New View: From the Inside Out...

Our Brain Constructs Our Reality! Contrary to our belief that we experience the physical world externally, cutting-edge neuroscience paints a different picture. Will Storr has some answers to the question of what reality 'actually' is:

"The world we experience as 'out there' is actually a reconstruction of reality that is built inside our heads. It's an act of creation by the storytelling brain. This is how it works. You walk into a room. Your brain predicts what the scene should look

and sound and feel like, then it generates a hallucination based on these predictions. It's this hallucination that you experience as the world around you. It's this hallucination you exist at the centre of, every minute of every day. You'll never experience actual reality because you have no direct access to it. […]

The job of all the senses is to pick up clues from the outside world in various forms: light waves, changes in air pressure, chemical signals. That information is translated into millions of tiny electrical pulses. Your brain reads these electrical pulses, in effect, like a computer reads code. It uses that code to actively construct your reality, fooling you into believing this controlled hallucination is real. It then uses its senses as fact-checkers, rapidly tweaking what it's showing you whenever it detects something unexpected. […]

There's no color out there either. Atoms are colorless. All the colors we do 'see' are a blend of three cones that sit in the eye: red, green and blue. This makes us Homo sapiens relatively impoverished members of the animal kingdom: some birds have six cones; mantis shrimp have sixteen; bees' eyes are able to see the electromagnetic structure of the sky. The colorful worlds they experience beggar human imagination. Even the colors we do 'see' are mediated by culture. Russians are raised to see two types of blue and, as a result, see eight-striped rainbows. […]

The only thing we'll ever really know are those electrical pulses that are sent up by our senses. Our storytelling brain uses those pulses to create a colorful set in which to play out our lives. It populates that set with a cast of actors with goals and personalities and finds plots for us to follow." [1]

The Director of the Institute of Neuroscience, David McCormick, explains, *"The human brain ... creates models of the world through information indirectly received from the senses. It analyzes quickly, making best guesses, and is prone to slipping up. It's easy to see where it can go wrong in sensory systems. Optical and auditory illusions are obvious examples.*

While the brain creates models of the physical world, it also makes models of a person's emotional, cultural and social worlds. These models are also created through shortcuts and best guesses, but the resulting illusions — or biases — can be much harder to spot." [2]

As Anil Seth, Professor of Neuroscience at the University of Sussex, says, *"... the idea of controlled hallucination [...] applies to everything that we perceive, and not just perceptions of things out there in the world, but also, it applies to our perceptions of our self, of our body, of our memories, of our sense of agency, of our sense of volition - that everything that we perceive is a construction".* [3]

When I really let these scientific findings in, they will completely rock my world.

My complete life is created from the inside out. We experience a movie in our brain, and our 5 senses just confirm the story. And it feels very, very real.

FACT! Our brain gets information via electrical pulses and creates a controlled hallucination. **What if I live in a complete hallucination?!**

There is actually no color or sound per se in the universe: **each brain creates a different model of the physical world.**

We only really think/feel we know us and what is happening in the world around us.

Our brain is the core of our human existence. **The complete film is created here. Our complete existence might be a big projection.** We have no proof that others even exist, outside our brains hallucination. And a very big part of this hallucination in us, is that this hallucination is only so cemented because everybody seems to watch a similar movie. For example: We all believe strongly in the power of money.

FACT! All of our different experiences, from happy to traumatic, are just happening in different areas in our brain.

These scientific revelations parallel the insights of ancient Indian sages:

"You are the cosmos and the cosmos is you. The cosmos is a projection of our divinity."

So, I ask you directly: What if depression, frustration, and misery, which seem so real in the movie of our lives, are merely constructs in a part of our brain? Could we not open ourselves to the "reality of enlightenment, bliss, and love" by accessing another part of our brain?

The center of our spirituality: The Parietal Cortex

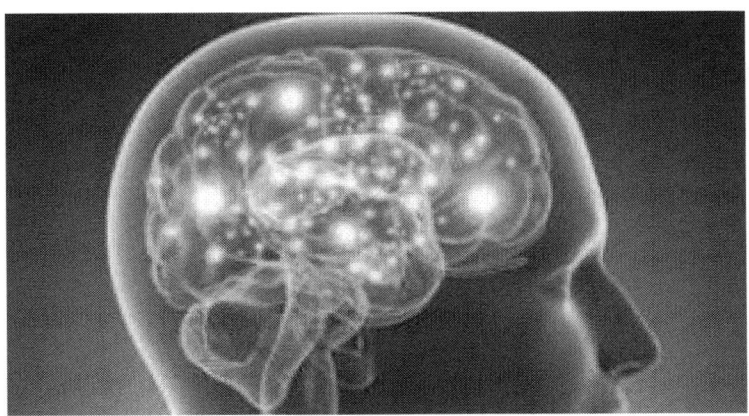

According to Marc Potenza, a psychiatry professor at Yale University, the 'Parietal Cortex' in the human brain associated with spirituality.

Transcendence, which is the ability to transcend one's own self, is also associated with spirituality.

The question isn't merely whether there is life after death but whether there is genuine life, free from illusion, before death—a life liberated from the shackles of fear, trauma, and survival.

Chapter 3

Quantum Physics: Enlightenment is just a glimpse away

My invitation in this chapter is to shift your perception in your brain from that of a cold and dangerous universe, in which you can be hit by cars, attacked by bears, and left by lovers, to a warm, mystical, magical, wondrous universe which you are part of and feel deeply connected to.

Most of us grew up learning from our parents, our culture, and from school about a cold universe, which is completely separate from us. We learn in physics that our world contains objects (of which our body is one) and these objects are subject to Newton's mechanical laws such as gravity.

In reality the universe is completely made out of the same mystical and magical substance that we and all form are made of, and at the deepest, truest level is completely unified; we can rest being home in this oneness.

"Yes, all things are made of atoms, and all atoms are made of the same three basic particles - protons, neutrons, and electrons."[4]
Keith Welch, Radiological Controls Group

This is exactly what we find when we look and enter into the spaciousness of our 'smaller' universe; our personal limited realities seem to dissolve.
And when we look into the real 'bigger' universe, the incredible vastness of time and space in our universe, our personal limited realities seem to dissolve as well.

> *"This information has the potential to dismantle our perceived self-centeredness and self-importance when we realize that we are basically empty space with lots of opinions and concepts about life and ourselves!"*

The Spaciousness of the Smaller

Let's look at the tiny building blocks of our universe:
Atoms are made out of even smaller protons, neutrons and electrons, all whirling and dancing around at super high speed. Entering our universe on the level of the atom you have basically just **vast empty space.** It is this high-speed movement of electrons that gives the atom the feeling of real matter.

To give you an idea of scale and proportions, imagine a tiny atom being the size of a big European cathedral or a sports arena like Madison Square Garden. At its centre would be a proton, the size of an orange, with a ping pong ball-sized electron flying around it. All the rest is empty space!

Hydrogen atoms make up more than 90 percent of all existing atoms (and three-quarters of the mass) of the universe.[5] A hydrogen atom is about 99.9999999999996% empty space. This means that everything in the universe – all form, yours, mine, everything single object – is almost completely empty space. [6]

Isn't this magical?

This information has the potential to dismantle our perceived self-centeredness and self-importance, if we realize that we are basically empty space with lots of opinions and concepts about life and ourselves!

A Multiverse of Probabilities

Our minds begin to crumble away even further when we look at what kind of crazy stuff happens on the sub-atomic level, all of which exists in us.

The basic principles of quantum mechanics lead us into a dimension of magical paradoxes and mystery which is clearly the opposite of our old and outdated models of Newton's physics that portraits a cold, loveless universe, where survival must be fought for.

"... you have the latent ability to jump like an electron from a state of inner self misery into a state of divine bliss!"

Robert Coolman states, *"In classical mechanics, objects exist in a specific place at a specific time. However, in quantum mechanics, objects instead exist in a haze of probability; they have a certain chance of being at point A, another chance of being at point B and so on."*[7]

Nobel prize winner Werner Heisenberg states that particles can exist at different places at the same time.

Following this train of thought we have the latent ability to jump like an electron from a state of inner self misery (in one part of our brain) into a state of divine bliss (in the Parietal Cortex)!

"You are, on your physical level of existence, dancing, magical energy full of miracles and wonders."

Chapter 4

The Stars are Calling Us Home

Life is all about perspective

We are eternal, infinite, unconditional love.
I love to take time to completely shift my awareness into the largest perspective possible.

The reality of us is eternal.
The reality of us is infinite.

Realizing this truth is so relaxing and immensely liberating. Taking the time to shift our awareness into the broadest perspective possible is a profound journey.
Opening up to the grandest and most expansive possibilities is a true gift.

Consider these astonishing scientific facts: NASA's latest data reveals the existence of 3,916 solar systems similar to ours within the Milky Way. Each of these systems contains stars with their own planets, including our sun, Earth with its moon, and celestial bodies like Mars and Saturn.

Moreover, experts suggest that there are approximately 200 billion galaxies in the observable universe, while some astronomers estimate a staggering 2 trillion galaxies in the entire universe. And, astonishingly, some scientists propose that our universe may be infinite.

As subtle spiritual beings, we have the capacity to connect with and open ourselves to this incredible vastness within us.
This profound shift transcends our self-centeredness and ushers in spaciousness, love, and genuine freedom.

The Stars Are Calling Us Home

Chapter 5
The Reality of Enlightenment and the Kingdom of God

The Paradise of God.

Perfect, complete love, bliss, and light exist within us.

It is a state free from lack, need, or self-judgment—a realm of pure being.

This existence is accessible at all times and in all places, with nothing to gain or lose.

Why does it exist? Because we can imagine it. Because we have all experienced it at some point in our lives.

Enlightenment, bliss, love, and light—these words and the realities they point to may be met with skepticism by many. Only a few resonate with them, and fewer still embark on the quest for their realization.

Here's the key revelation: Your self does not need to change at all. The belief in change, transformation, improvement, higher or lower energies, or even dark entities can divert us from entering the paradise of love within.

Ultimately, the reality of enlightenment hinges entirely on our extraordinary **power of belief**.

Throughout our lives, we seek deep fulfillment and strive to enhance our well-being with every action. We first believe that simple pleasures like a delicious snack or coffee bring fulfillment. Then we chase happiness in material possessions such as money, cars, and houses. The love for pets follows, followed by intense and sometimes tumultuous love for our partners, spouses, and families. We eventually enter the realm of spirituality, exploring meditation groups and seeking spiritual guidance.

In all our pursuits, we are still ensnared in the **duality and projection game**. As long as we project our happiness, love, and wisdom onto entities outside of ourselves, we cannot fully realize the paradise of being. It's simply not possible.

Herein lies the cosmic irony: We think we must change our selves first to become "enlightened" and bathe in divine, unconditional love. We believe we must be perpetually happy and harbor only loving, kind thoughts and feelings toward ourselves and others before we can claim enlightenment and knowledge of God. Paradoxically, these conditional thoughts and feelings keep us from embracing divine love—a true Catch-22!

From a scientific perspective, you can access the Parietal Cortex, the center of spirituality in your brain, and experience a sense of flow, peace, and relaxation after or during practices like meditation, prayer, or yoga.

As we learned in Chapter 2, modern brain research confirms that our entire life's movie is created from within our brains. In our outdated worldview, we were conditioned to be victims, perceiving life as mostly happening from the outside in. We believed that our senses picked up stimuli from the external world, leading to our reactions in the form of thoughts and feelings. However, this thinking is antiquated.

When we allow ourselves to embrace new thinking, we open ourselves to the possibility of believing in any reality we construct within our brains. Thus, by opening up to the reality of enlightenment—a full immersion in divine happiness, bliss, and delight—we eventually experience it. It is the loftiest reality that humans can aspire to.

It represents the ultimate goal and state of being we can attain.

If we acknowledge that all our actions, whether conscious or unconscious, are fundamentally driven by a pursuit of happiness or well-being, why not connect directly to and immerse ourselves in the source of our existence?

You chose THIS, and THIS will choose YOU!

At the outset of your journey, you may choose to dedicate time in the early morning and late evening to embark on your direct exploration. The method you choose doesn't matter; meditation is simply sitting and contemplating. Engaging in deep breathing, singing, or praying serves as a high-level inner dialogue you initiate within yourself, as our bodies are instruments of vibration. In my experience, this journey knows no end.

If you encounter resistance or discomfort in your brain or body, it may be rooted in past traumatic experiences. Consider bilateral stimulation or EMDR therapy. Personally, I find solace in listening to the sounds of nature and spiritual chants through headphones, even in the cold Canadian winter.

Some days, you might find me sitting outside in the early hours of the morning at 4 or 5 a.m., savoring life to the fullest. I cherish it immensely.

The beauty lies in realizing that there's nothing to achieve because in this spiritual reality, there is only the source of unconditional love we all yearn for.

This is the book's fundamental message: The reality of enlightenment is independent of the state of our self. Any expectations or desires for self-change are steps in the wrong

direction. How can we enter the realm of perfect love when we hold expectations about how we (and others) should be?

First, let's open ourselves to the possibility of enlightenment, bathed in light and love. Then, let's embrace love without conditions, starting with ourselves. Anyone who tells you that you should be different is manipulating and abusing you.

Believe, believe, believe!

Belief moves mountains.

Chapter 6

The Reality of Receiving God/Love/Bliss

It is always available for you.

It carries no conditions or prerequisites.

Often, we harbor thoughts and feelings of inadequacy, believing we are not worthy of love and enlightenment. However, the entrance into the kingdom of God imposes **no requirements** related to your

appearance,

body weight,

health,

mental or emotional state,

religion,

self-love or self-hate,

frustration,

depression,

achievements,

bank account,

or relationship status.

What aids in accessing your space of enlightenment?
1. **Quiet, Comfortable Moments:** Spend time sitting warmly and comfortably in the early morning and/or before bedtime.

2. **Deepest, Relaxing Breathing:** Experiment with gentle pauses between inhaling and exhaling. Ancient Indian sages suggest that the entry into God occurs between two breaths, two thoughts, and two actions.

3. **Bilateral Stimulation:** Listen to nature sounds with headphones. You can find scientific evidence of its therapeutic potential by researching EMDR therapy.

4. **"Living Affirmations" in Inner Dialogue:** Living affirmations are a form of fresh inner dialogue in which you confirm what you already know and experience within yourself. For instance, affirm that "I am warmly accepting whatever I feel inside right now", "I am completely in love with real enlightenment" or that "I am entering the core of God now."

Difference Between "Dead Affirmations" and "Living Affirmations":

a. **Duality:** Many prayers maintain duality, implying a separation between you and God/love/light. This separation is not true, regardless of deeply ingrained concepts and beliefs.

b. **Meaningless Repetition:** Some prayers become meaningless repetitions.

c. **Material Desires:** Some people seek material things through prayer and become frustrated with their spiritual progress. Deep within our hearts, we are less concerned with the material world and more interested in profound meaning.

Endless debates about the existence of God, the creation of the cosmos, and potential mistakes in creation often overshadow the quiet, subtle bliss within us. By dedicating time daily to our beloved, blissful core, the experience of ultimate, infinite, eternal light/love/bliss within us will grow, even if we occasionally feel otherwise.

The concept of "I am enlightened," meaning that one is always blissful and happy, can be very misleading. Being on this planet in a physical body means we are connected to the human experience, which includes the "perceived pain of the world." There is no escaping the reality of cutting and being cut by others.

However, alongside our human experience exists the reality of enlightenment—an open invitation to attain the highest meaning available in this universe.

How can we achieve it? First warmly accepting our emotional state on the inside, and then clearly ceasing the projection and outsourcing game and recognizing that our core is ecstatic love, which requires no conditions to manifest itself.

We don't have to conform to specific standards in ourselves before we can fully embrace complete love.

Chapter 7

The Projection Game

The question of whether we genuinely desire to receive enlightenment or if we prefer holding onto our deeply ingrained belief systems, often referred to as "holy cows," is a profound one.

What are Holy Cows? Holy cows are those belief systems that are so deeply rooted that we are willing to defend them staunchly. One of the most significant holy cows is the "Projection Game," which involves the outsourcing of our love and happiness.

Many of us, if we are honest, seek and depend on our partners, children, pets, or spiritual teachers to make us happy. However, this belief perpetually keeps us from realizing the source of true happiness and enlightenment.

So, how can we shift from being stuck in our human experience to enjoying bathing in bliss and love?

Dependency from Childhood: From infancy, we humans are deeply enmeshed in the 'Projection Game.' We literally receive nourishment and love from the outside world in the form of mother's milk. Our well-being is heavily dependent on the care and presence of our parents during our upbringing. This dependency becomes deeply ingrained in our DNA.

The Path to Adulthood and Enlightenment: As we mature, we embark on a journey toward 'real' adulthood, which equates to

enlightenment. Becoming adults means allowing ourselves to discern what is real and what is illusion, doesn't it?
Ancient Indian sages have long asserted that the phenomenal world is a grand illusion, often referred to as Maya. Quantum physics teaches us that the universe is primarily empty space, with high-frequency particles creating the illusion of solid matter.

The Illusory Nature of Reality: Our five senses confirm the narrative of our life, which appears very real. Yet, this seemingly real story dissolves every night during deep sleep and seems to vanish entirely when our physical body ceases to exist.

Could it be that our brain is a grand projector that casts light and love onto the people and objects in our life's movie, also known as 'my reality/life'?
I can see that throughout my life, I projected my love, wisdom, and happiness onto others because I believed in the human mantra, 'I am not good enough.' Once I fully realize this, I must conclude: No more projection, outsourcing, or leakage of love, wisdom, truth, and bliss onto other human beings. The more I project, the less I can realize within myself—does that make sense?

The Power of Intention: Our minds have incredible power. What we set our minds and hearts to can eventually become our reality, whether positively or negatively. Setting our focus on the source of well-being, bliss, and happiness will lead to its realization.
Believe, believe, believe.

The Most Important Message: The core message of this book is to cease the projection game entirely and stop outsourcing our love. This doesn't mean leaving your partner, family, or changing your life. It's an invitation to be honest and acknowledge and embrace lovingly what we are all doing 24/7.

The Deep Pain and Connection: On a physical level, there is often a sense of lacking love and feeling unworthy of God's love. This is a fundamental aspect of our human experience. We are always connected to each other, both in joy and suffering. However, there's a fine line between sharing love and becoming overly dependent on external sources for it.

The Ultimate Realization:
The key realization is that all existing love, bliss, and happiness in the universe can only be found within. The more we outsource this divine love to external sources, the further we distance ourselves from it. Meditation, among other practices, teaches us to draw our senses inward, cease projecting our light externally, and allow divine light and energy to flourish within us. **The abundant love of the divine awaits us within.**

We love to really realize that all existing love, bliss, and happiness in this universe can only be found inside.

The more I outsource this divine love to anybody or anything, the more I separate myself from it.

In meditation we learn to draw the senses in, we stop projecting our light outside of us, so the divine light and energy can grow inside. God with its abundant love is awaiting us on the inside.

Chapter 8

We Are The Miracle

"You are of divine inheritance. You are complete, nothing is missing. There is only love existing in truth."

You are of divine inheritance, complete, lacking nothing. Truth reveals that only love exists.

Our Innate Innocence: We are profoundly innocent beings of the Divine, regardless of our circumstances:

It doesn't matter if you find solace in something as seemingly innocuous as a cup of coffee or a piece of chocolate, or if you've struggled with more challenging addictions like sex and drug abuse, or even harmful actions toward yourself and others. It doesn't matter how you perceive your appearance or self-worth.

The 'Kingdom of God,' characterized by pure forgiveness, warm acceptance, tender love, deep fulfillment, and ecstatic bliss, is ALWAYS and EVERYWHERE available to EVERYONE, at ANY TIME.

Why?
- It's rooted in the very essence of unconditional, eternal love itself.
- You are born out of and into the mystical miracle of love: billions of atoms come together in a cosmic dance to manifest your existence and the intricate story of your life.
- As conscious beings, we possess the incredible capacity to be like the particles in Quantum physics: existing in different states simultaneously. In one part of our brain, we may feel lonely, frustrated, sad, and unworthy, while in another part, we are blissful, happy, and deeply fulfilled, beings of light and love. A shift is always possible!

Whatever helps us transcend energy and consciousness levels, we cherish and cultivate: whether it's yoga, profound affirmation, meditation, conscious breathing, bilateral stimulation, dancing, or any practice that elevates our consciousness.

Switching and transcending energy levels is akin to building a muscle. Initially, it may feel unfamiliar and challenging, but with practice, it becomes more natural and effortless.

Ultimately, it's the most authentic journey: originating from love, we search for genuine love until we realize that we have always been love within ourselves.
It's the most profound journey of our lives.

Chapter 9

The Human Experience And the Divine Experience

"See, embrace, love, integrate, and transcend the human experience."

But what is the **human experience**?

It encompasses all the intense emotions we, as human beings, feel, except for the highest feeling of God, which is bliss, light, and ultimate love.

Our day-to-day human life experience is often characterized by underlying stress, fear, anger, and anxiety deeply ingrained in our body's cells. These feelings are occasionally balanced by brief interludes of rest during sleep, exercise, moments of connection in conversation, and the enjoyment of delicious foods and drinks.

This is the human experience, and within it lies the **human predicament**. There's no escaping the human experience as long as we inhabit a physical body, energetically connected to this planet within its actual unique energetic framework:

We, the people, lie, betray, abuse, hurt, and even kill each other. It's a reflection of the world we live in.

Also, contemplating the "cruelty" of Mother Nature often leads us to witness both the stunning beauty and the brutal reality of the natural world. For instance, imagine the powerful but heart-wrenching sight of hungry lions tearing apart a helpless newborn deer. Observing such an event can evoke a profound and poignant feeling within our body.

Our most significant human challenge is our constant evaluation, judgment, and comparison of ourselves to others.

We believe: "I should be thinner or heavier, smarter, richer, happier, nicer, and so on..."

We think we must attain these conditions before we can love ourselves, receive love, and find happiness.

For those on a spiritual path, it means letting go of these seemingly endless conditions and comparisons to supposedly higher-evolved teachers—a great illusion in itself.

These self-judgments are the painful expulsion from paradise. They represent some of the most profound and challenging addictions we face as humans.

Most people have a significant misunderstanding of the term 'forgiveness.' With a Christian background, we're taught to forgive our neighbors for wronging us. While there's merit in opening our hearts with empathy and learn to forgive others, this concept can lead to judgment, arrogance, and self-importance, as we, in an act of 'greatness,' forgive others for their sins.

In the state of divine bliss, there's no need for forgiveness, nor a need to receive it.

To me, the most crucial aspect of forgiveness pertains only to oneself. We've all been conditioned with strong concepts of right, wrong, good, evil, and sin.

Judging ourselves harshly is deeply ingrained in our DNA. We often believe:

"I should look different, I should eat less, I should eat healthier, I should work out more, I should make more money, My house should be nicer, I should be nicer, I should have more friends, I should be more peaceful, I should be loved by my family, I should be enlightened."

These thoughts and intense emotions swim in our human minds as part of the system on this planet.

I see it, I feel it, and when I catch myself believing in it, the divine invitation is to **deeply and completely forgive myself for doing so. This opens our heart and love begins to flow again.**

Return home to the freshest, sweetest, dearest, and all-encompassing love within. A love so profound and encompassing that when we enter it, there's no one left to forgive.

Just as with any addiction, we can find something more appealing and fulfilling than the addiction itself in order to let go and heal. Transitioning into divine bliss and light becomes a beautiful and deeply satisfying **new addiction**.

Speaking of the human experience, what about the divine experience?

It's a state of perfect elevation, pure bliss, and an ecstatic flow of love. In this state, there is no space or time. It's independent and intrinsic, requiring no external stimuli.

We humans get to experience both: the human and the divine. It seems essential to realize that the human and the divine experience are one.

Both may feel very different at times, so how can we bridge the perceived gap? My way is to feel deeply, accept and embrace completely, and love fully what's inside. Whatever needs to be seen, felt, embraced, and loved—be it anger, hatred, frustration, pain, desperation, or sadness—we learn to embrace even the seemingly unembraceable.

Any feeling can be present, REALLY!

This small act of embrace is the gateway to the oneness of the divine experience. With it, I can fully enter the divine, even despite all these negative emotions.

The divine is eternal, infinite love without boundaries. You don't need to look or be a certain way to access the realm of God.

If our pain and trauma patterns are too strong, professional therapies like EMDR and IFS can be beneficial. It's essential to keep our focus on the target: the reality of receiving enlightenment, which is always there, waiting for us to enter, no matter how desperate we may feel.

Why? Bliss, ecstasy, and love must be inside because, at some point in our lives, we've experienced these feelings internally, no matter how strongly we believe they come from external sources. Scientifically, we all have a Parietal Cortex, a spiritual center, in our brains.

Some may argue that therapy is the only way and that seeking spiritual enlightenment might be an escape from facing and feeling the darker aspects within us. While this can be the case, only honesty and self-love can pave the path to 'real enlightenment.' Nothing else truly works and ultimately satisfies.

At our core, we are God in Oneness. As we move into physical form we enter the realm of duality. We become the creators of both inside and outside. And we are all consciously and unconsciously in love with the transcendental experience and feeling of our core, God.

Observe intoxicated soccer fans cheering for their team or music lovers attending a concert. They are all seeking the experience of deep transcendental love all day long.

When you honestly contemplate the origins of your addictions, you'll find that, in following these cravings, you seek to return to the beautiful, ecstatic, and unconditional love of the all-encompassing Father/Mother principle. Coming back home into the divine is the only thing that truly satisfies our hunger for love.

If you are genuinely interested in the flow of divine ecstasy and bliss, you must open your eyes fully and acknowledge the human experience for what it is.

Then, gently do the inner work to enter the divine experience within.

Nobody, absolutely nobody, can do that for you!

It might seem as though you can experience this through a lover, friend, therapist, or spiritual teacher, but that is not true freedom. It's still playing the game of dependency and projection, like a child.

Since the dawn of human existence, there has been a resounding invitation to enter the divine flow of eternal and infinite bliss. Few people answer the call to become true adults and gaze directly into the reality of receiving enlightenment.

You can.

While everyone looks for happiness outside, we sit on the pot of gold waiting within us. Meditation, deep breathing with pauses between inhales and exhales, high-level affirmations/prayers, and bilateral stimulation—all these practices really work.

Ask yourself: What do I truly, truly want right now? What do I genuinely need right now?

There is only entering the highest love, bliss, God, or enlightenment with all that you have at this very moment.

Chapter 10

Self Acceptance

Deep within us all lies a profound awareness of perfect, unconditional love and acceptance—a gentle, warm current of love. We yearn for it, strive towards it, wish for it, pray for it, and often, even unconsciously, expect this love from others.

Having this intimate knowledge of complete, perfect love within, we embark on a grand projection, assuming that our own selves, our bodies, all the people around us, and the world at large should embody this "perfect love."

It is essential to acknowledge an undeniable truth: in our current state of humanity, our individual selves are far from perfect, and they should never be, nor can they ever be perfect. Warmly embracing this reality in its entirety is of utmost importance. Changing the world, humanity, is much, much too big of a task for our limited selves.

And our human potential is remarkable: an ever-present, subtle stream of perfect, fulfilling love resides within the Parietal Cortex, awaiting our discovery when we turn our five senses inward.

Within the human experience, countless perfect imperfections and flaws exist—both within us and within others. The stress and pressure we inflict on ourselves and those around us by not accepting our inherent imperfections is substantial.

I firmly believe in healing through acceptance rather than attempting to willfully change ourselves and others. Our journey involves continuously practicing the art of being this inner love, embracing our perfect imperfections within ourselves, and extending that love towards everyone we encounter.

It's imperative to recognize that individuals, particularly religious leaders and teachers who preach self-betterment or claim to have attained perfection, are often deceiving themselves and others. Their motive may be to wield power over you, making you feel inadequate. This is one of the oldest and darkest forms of manipulation, aimed at capturing your attention, money, and sex.

The concept of self-improvement, or the idea that someone is superior or inferior to you, is a grand illusion. Conversely, the concept of self-acceptance and self-love is profoundly real and indispensable.

The journey begins within: I wholeheartedly advocate for complete self-love and acceptance as a prerequisite before seeking such all-encompassing love from others. I embrace my darkness and imperfections with love.

As I wholeheartedly accept my imperfections, negative emotions, physical limitations, and perceived faults, a genuine, warm wellspring of love and acceptance blossoms from within. In this space, we find inner peace and love, replacing inner turmoil.

The more skilled I become at this form of self-embrace, the less I yearn for external validation and confirmation.

We are all inherently innocent beings of the Divine. Whether we grapple with addictions to coffee, chocolate, food, TV, substances, work, money, material possessions, or relationships, or whether we have committed hurtful actions towards ourselves and others, as we all may have at some point, we can warmly and wholeheartedly embrace our darkness and imperfections.

The Kingdom of God, characterized by forgiveness, warm acceptance, tender love, deep fulfillment, and ecstatic bliss, is eternally and universally accessible on the inside to all, at any given moment. Why? Because it springs from the intrinsic existence of unconditional, eternal love itself.

We emerge from and into the miraculous realm of love, where billions of atoms converge and dance to orchestrate our existence and the intricate narrative of our lives.

In a parallel perspective, akin to Quantum physics, particles exhibit the remarkable property of simultaneous existence at multiple locations. Similarly, we may find ourselves perceiving one aspect of our existence as a lonesome, frustrated, and melancholic state, while concurrently experiencing another dimension of our being as a blissful, joyful, and profoundly excited being of light and love.

We can nurture the ability to shift between these energy levels and states of being through practices like yoga, high-level prayer, meditation, deep conscious breathing, bilateral stimulation, and dance. This transformation mirrors the process of muscle training—initially feeling unfamiliar and challenging but progressively improving with continued practice.

Ultimately, this journey represents the most authentic love relationship: a journey originating from love, where we ardently seek genuine love until we recognize that we have always been love itself. It is the most rewarding voyage of our lives.

Chapter 11

Our Mind, The Golden Retriever

Have you ever noticed how our minds constantly seem to crave something? It's as if they're running an endless program, always in pursuit, retrieval, and achievement mode. I find it akin to the enthusiasm of a golden retriever dog that loves fetching things thrown by its owner.

Our mind/brain program might be seeking:
- A million dollars
- The perfect dream partner
- The ideal career
- The perfect body

- The flawless house
- The ultimate car
- The perfect orgasm
- The ideal drug
- The perfect food or drink
- The ideal therapy, healing, relief from trauma

Additionally, the mind program appears to have a penchant for focusing on negative experiences, trauma, and drama. Some spiritual teachings advocate achieving a state of no mind, but, to my understanding, this seems unattainable given the active and resilient nature of the mind.

Other teachers claim to attain inner silence. In another chapter of this book, I humorously address these teachers because they employ their minds, thoughts and voices, breaking their "holy silence" to instruct their students to be silent. It's quite mystical!

However, here's an intriguing question: Is it genuinely about the objects of our desire, or is it about the feelings associated with achieving or experiencing those goals?

If we're entirely honest with ourselves, we'll recognize that everything we think and do throughout the day aims to improve our well-being. Our efforts are geared toward approaching profound happiness, fulfillment, and the highest states of ecstasy and bliss. It's rarely about the specific objects of our desire; it's consistently about the emotions we anticipate when we reach our desired goals.

I'm not suggesting that you should abandon all your life goals. Instead, I want to introduce the possibility that what we truly long for is deep happiness and fulfillment, brimming with love and bliss. When we reside in that state of childlike joy and profound contentment, the significance of the material world diminishes, doesn't it?

If your answer is yes, then why not embark directly on the journey to your inner source of happiness? The parietal cortex is the epicenter of our spirituality, inviting us to enter.

Ask yourself: What do I genuinely wish to attain and experience right now? What do I truly love doing at this moment?

For me, the answer is always the same: I yearn to access the purest source of love itself. I love to feel the effervescent pearls of bliss bubbling within my mind. Nothing else can truly satisfy me at my core.

It's as if you've tasted the most exquisite champagne, and now, all you crave is that champagne; nothing else will suffice. You cannot settle for anything less.

The most wonderful news is that the best emotional state you can ever find is within you, and it's even free. We literally sit upon the source of this incredible bliss, and we can meld with it.

As humans, we harbor countless addictions: to food, drinks, drugs, work, money, power, sex, and more. Instead of engaging in constant battles and struggles with these addictions, consider **embracing them wholeheartedly. Then, contemplate creating a new addiction: the pursuit of something more rewarding, nourishing, and delightful—dive into the bliss of your inner existence by turning your five senses inward.**

Let's consider using the mind for its divine function: Entering, manifesting, and enjoying God-Space. Instead of battling the mind over negativity, we can give it its true function: thinking as God from the Parietal Cortex—divine thoughts in a divine conversation, created by the highest within.
We love to learn to think like God thinks: We can create thoughts full of enjoyment, love, acknowledgement, fulfillment, bliss, and deep happiness.
Breathe deeply, relax, and engage in a loving, high-level conversation with yourself. You can create anything. Anything your human mind can conceive, you can manifest.

Take the time before and after night sleep to turn your senses inward through meditation:
1. Recognize that we are beings of frequency, influenced by sound and words. Create a high-level inner conversation, prayer, or affirmation that elevates your spirit and allows you to soar.
2. Practice deep breathing, bringing life-giving oxygen into your body. If you like, experiment with briefly holding your breath after inhaling, as ancient Indian Rishis suggested that the gateway to the Divine lies between two breaths. Breathe deeply for your eternal life.
3. Listen to beautiful music and soothing nature sounds with headphones, stimulating both the left and right hemispheres of your brain to support your healing journey.

Chapter 12

Transformation and Transcendence

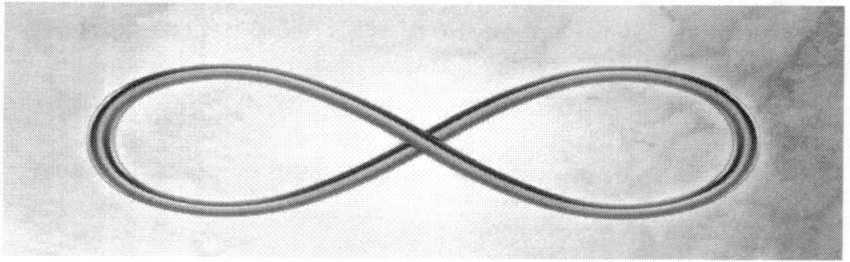

The term "transcendence" signifies rising above a limited, earthly-bound self and ascending into a higher state of consciousness that is beyond reach or touch. "Transformation," on the other hand, refers to a thorough or dramatic change in form or appearance.

The symbol of the figure-eight, which resembles the sign of eternity and eternal growth, represents the continuous cycles of our potential for personal growth.

We are beckoned into the transcendent realm of divine happiness, joy, and bliss that surpasses all conventional human experiences. We take delight in wholeheartedly entering a state of love, much like an innocent child of God, detached from our ego and identity. It's akin to a ecstatic, complete reset or restart of our life and our connection with the world, all while remaining fully awake. In this state, all our personal stories fade away, and we immerse ourselves in the embrace of our divine essence.

Then, just a moment later, we find ourselves back in the human experience—engaging in interactions with others, experiencing the cuts and bruises of the human experience, feeling vulnerable, bleeding, and aching. This is the human experience, reminding us that pain is an inherent part of inhabiting a body on this planet.

We humans are vulnerable, experience pain, and suffer. This is a reminder from the divine that there will always be challenges and suffering while we inhabit a physical body on this planet without its complete transformation.

Yet, we return to the realm of unconditional love within us, reestablishing our connection with the divine, and once again experiencing the touch of God.
However, this time, the connection goes a little deeper, with an increased flow of love and a greater sense of inner peace.

This is an ongoing cycle within us, a growing circle of inner joy and fulfillment as we come to know the ultimate beauty and love within ourselves, leading to profound healing and transformation.

Chapter 13

The Purpose of Our Life and the Idea of the Ideal

What if the reality of enlightenment is indeed attainable in our lives?
What if there exists an inner realm where abundance flows like milk and honey?
What if an eternal divine ecstasy is an ever-present experience within us?

For those who are intrigued by the highest potential of our human existence, I invite you to embark on your own exploration.

Ask for the Highest, and it shall be granted to you. You!

What stands as the most deceptive obstacle to entering the kingdom of God?
The notion of self-improvement: the belief that we must first enhance, purify, and transform ourselves to fully accept and love who we are. This belief extends to the expectation of receiving love from our partners and families only after we have altered ourselves to fit an idealized image of self.
Let us not confine ourselves to the limitations of our day-to-day survival existence, characterized by the fight-or-flight response. Instead, let us step boldly into the transcendental realm of bliss,

light, and ecstasy at the very core of God, where our entire existence finds its purpose.

What holds me back?

Thoughts and intense emotions that dictate, "I should be different. I should not experience negativity, anger, sadness, or frustration. I should look better, lose weight, and so on."
Our notions and ideals of a vastly improved self seem to be deeply ingrained in our minds. This illusion perpetuates the ceaseless suffering stemming from the stark contrast between reality and this idealized self-image. Out of this ongoing comparison arises the conviction: "I am not good enough; I am not worthy."

This very illusion is what keeps us from entering the state of perfect love within, the realm of God.

So, what can I do to find my way back home to God?
I passionately desire to make peace with myself, to fully embrace my being as it is—unchanged and unaltered. In that moment of genuine self-realization, I can wholly surrender to who I am. In this moment, I immerse myself in the boundless stream of divine bliss, love, and ecstasy. We are utterly adored by the cosmos.
This is one of the grandest cosmic jokes and a perfect paradox: I believe I must transform into perfect love to become what I already am within my parietal cortex—a being of perfect love.
We must learn to embrace ourselves entirely, just as we are, to relax, and to transcend into divine love.

Of course, we reside in these bodies, which are perpetually connected to the human experience, rife with limitations, pain, and frustration. As far as my knowledge extends, there is no escape from this human experience while inhabiting a physical form.

Returning from these experiences, I may perhaps begin to judge myself, and at that point, I must once again love myself with the encompassing divine love that knows no bounds. It's all about love and acceptance.

We find ourselves traversing both realms—human and divine—going in and out of the divine, and recognizing that it's perfectly okay to do so. There is the human experience, and there is the divine experience—Yin and Yang in perfect harmony.

Chapter 14

Complete Love

We are here to learn the art of complete love.

Our journey begins with inanimate objects such as houses, cars, diamonds, and gold bars. We attach value and affection to these possessions.

Next, we ascend to the animated world, where we find deep love for our beloved pets. Cats and dogs become cherished companions, and we lavish them with affection.

Then, we step into the complex and often perilous realm of human love. Many of us bear the scars of past hurts and traumas, so we cautiously open our hearts, but only to a limited extent. Perhaps you're in a marriage where you've given just enough to ensure your partner doesn't leave, but this cautious approach may leave you feeling unfulfilled.

Our hearts, however, are designed for complete love. Yet, this kind of love is not typically programmed into our human consciousness.

For me, complete love means giving endlessly on a deep spiritual level, regardless of the circumstances. It involves experiencing both being wounded and causing hurt to others due to our conditioned and limited selves, which operate on the basis of projections and expectations. Through this process, we endure pain, we can open for healing, and gradually allow more love to flow first within us and then outward.

In this journey, we naturally progress into the realm of divine love—an unlimited, unconditional, and eternal love.

Interestingly, some "spiritual individuals" believe they can skip levels and proclaim themselves to be in a state of divine love, but they often leave a trail of strained or broken relationships in their wake. Skipping levels doesn't truly work. If you're unsure of where you stand on this journey, you can always inquire about your level of realization from past partners, friends, or relationships that may have ended.

There is no judgment in this process. We can simply embrace our patterns with honesty and warmth.

Chapter 15

The Door To Our Paradise

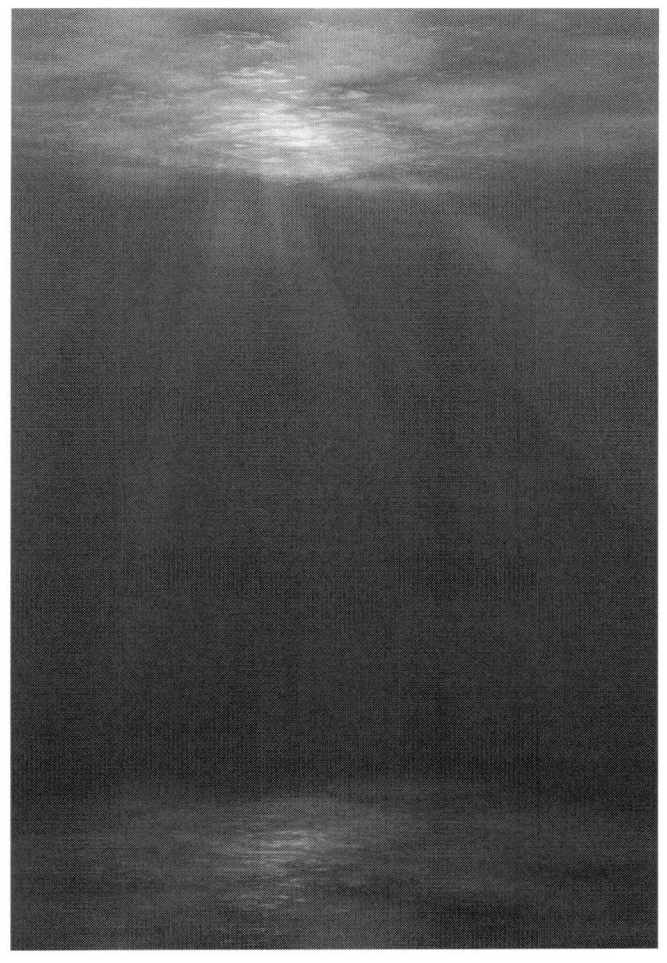

The door to inner paradise warmly invites us to acknowledge and embrace our deepest feelings.

On this planet, the usual tendency is to avoid acknowledging these profound emotions. We keep ourselves busy with countless projects, anything to evade the experience of deep feelings. Even noble pursuits such as truthfulness and spirituality can serve as distractions, keeping us away from that seemingly intimidating door.

Why do we do this?
Because behind that door may lie a vast ocean of emotions—sadness, loneliness, depression, shame, anger—that most people are understandably hesitant to confront. These feelings can appear immense and perilous, as they have the potential to pull us into dysfunction, mental disorders and even mental illnesses. Moreover, when we look at the external world, it often appears as an unending, intensifying stream of cruelty, greed for power and money, hatred, and war, which can feel overwhelmingly powerful.

On a side note: Our brains are wired to handle solvable problems in our personal lives, and they may struggle when confronted with unsolvable problems on a larger scale. The daily news often contains a significant amount of negative information, and many of the global issues it covers can indeed seem overwhelming and beyond our personal scope. Watching the news we see a lot of misery and suffering and while sitting our TV chair we are not able actually help, nor deal with our emotions in a good way. This phenomenon can lead to a sense of helplessness, anxiety, or even desensitization to the suffering of others, as individuals may feel powerless to make a meaningful impact on such vast and seemingly intractable problems. It's essential for individuals to find a balance between staying informed about important global issues and maintaining their mental and emotional well-being.

What can we do about our deepest and most challenging feelings of frustration, anger, and unworthiness?

Love is the only answer.
The path forward involves truly embracing these deep feelings, and most importantly, embracing ourselves. Full self-forgiveness is key. When you begin to embrace the seemingly "non-embraceable," you instantly reconnect with the flow of love. Pushing these feelings away or ignoring them is resistance, not love. These emotions may persist even after years of meditation or therapy; they cannot be pushed aside or rationalized away. Instead, we can offer them divine, eternal, all-encompassing love.

Imagine the perfect parents you wished for as a child—always present, caring, and loving. Now, you can begin to embody these perfect parents for yourself. All your feelings, even the darkest and deepest ones, want to be acknowledged, embraced, and loved. Revel in the freedom to fully embrace even your darkest emotions. Bilateral stimulation techniques like EMDR (Eye Movement Desensitization and Reprocessing) can be immensely helpful when touching upon the darkest feelings. Simply listening to soothing sounds like ocean waves for hours with headphones can also aid in this process. Additionally, seeking support from skilled therapists can be beneficial.

Ultimately, the profound emotion that comprises our essence is warm, tender, and boundless love.

Chapter 16

Transcendental Bliss

Transcendental bliss is our true nature and home.

Sometimes, the strong feeling of 'I am not worth it' or 'I am not good enough' may seem incredibly real. But it is the most significant lie on this planet! Let's stop feeding it.

All we really have as humans is the RIGHT NOW in this moment!

In this very moment, we are all completely perfect and absolutely innocent, like newborn babies.

Life has just started anew in this moment. Everything in this moment is new, fresh, and filled with unlimited possibilities.

Realize.

Deeper, relaxing, transcendental breathing is our ever-present, loving, reliable friend.

To love deeply with childlike love and ancient wisdom is our inextinguishable, unbreakable rocket fuel.

Let the already-written story unfold sweetly and gracefully.

Enjoy the ocean of love inside of us.

Chapter 17

The Function of a True "Spiritual Master"

You are the blissful giant of love and the embodiment of a true 'spiritual master.'

When you encounter a genuine 'teacher of truth', they will reveal to you the bliss and nourishing silence of G O D, which is the essential role of a spiritual teacher.

They should also immediately make it clear that the 'master-student' attachment relationship is the most significant and final illusory projection. Believing in it creates duality, separation, and eternal suffering.

Unfortunately, numerous spiritual teachers exist who thrive on the innocent ignorance of their students. Both teachers and students engage in an unending game of co-dependency:
The teacher gains a career, money, adoration, and, at times, even sexual intimacy with students for their services, while the student projects the perfect father/mother figure onto the teacher.

It is good to transcend this concept.
Certainly, we all desire to meet the ultimate, god-like, perfect Father/Mother figure who unconditionally loves, heals, and saves us. However, it doesn't work that way. Unfortunately, no one can delve into your innermost depths and heal your pain for you; you are the only one capable of that.

Moreover, no one can enter the irresistible bliss, joy, and peace of the Parietal Cortex, the spiritual center of your brain, on your behalf.

A true Master recognizes Oneness and refrains from creating any dependency or duality. They will not suggest that anyone on this planet, especially not themselves, possesses more love, light, or wisdom than you. A genuine master does not seek your money, adoration, power, or sexual intimacy in exchange for revealing the reality of unconditional, deep love.

The term 'spiritual teacher' is paradoxical: someone who claims to have realized 'oneness' or 'silence' creates instant duality by declaring themselves a 'special' and 'realized' teacher. A teacher who continuously teaches ignorant students, supposedly lacking 'God,' perpetuates a dark joke.

In the realm of true spirituality and enlightenment, we are all fundamentally on the same level. Everyone, even the 'divine' teacher, possesses an 'ego' on the human experience level, much like how everyone has a unique appearance.

Beware the big trap: 'My teacher is the embodiment of truth or is more realized than me.'
An example of this trap is when a spiritual teacher tells you that you must maintain silence to progress spiritually while simultaneously breaking their own silence by speaking about silence. This contradiction is absurd.

Our mind is a beautiful, divine instrument for attaining and expressing God-state.

We have all felt the divine, all-encompassing, ecstatic, unconditional love. We experienced it as babies, and we occasionally glimpse it in our lives.
Some call it the Truth.
The ultimate truth is that this experience and feeling can only be found within. Why? Because it resides within! Recent brain research designates the spiritual center of our brain as the Parietal Cortex.

We can share this divine love. It may appear to originate externally when we meditate or practice yoga with others or listen to a priest/teacher who reminds us.

However, it truly exists only within us when we are genuinely honest with ourselves. We create a profound inner dialogue of love, which grants us the divine love experience we yearn for. Therefore, you are the only one capable of realizing this love, regardless of any projected dependency on the teacher, partner, sex, dog, delicious foods/drinks, and so on.

In my understanding, a spiritual teacher or priest can remind you of your divinity, but they must be 100% clear that you can only access this diamond within through meditation, yoga, or high-level prayer.
It turns dark and abusive when the teacher:
a. Claims to be superior or more realized than everyone else. Such a declaration exposes their falseness because, as long as one inhabits a body, they are part of the human experience's vibrational tapestry.
b. Fails to teach their students how to independently access enlightenment, making it all about themselves and the requirement for physical proximity, thereby fostering an unhealthy dependency.

c. Converts their 'realization' into a lucrative business and asserts that attending their meetings is the only path to evolution.
d. Engages in sexual relationships with students who depend on them.

Sexuality has its place in our human existence as a means of reproduction. While it can also be a beautiful expression of physical love, we must remember that we are first and foremost spiritual beings without bodies. Spiritual movements and realizations always lead to a deeper connection with the divine. Sexual love may spring from that source, but it is not a prerequisite for evolving toward God; it can also become an addictive trap.

If you are following a teacher, here are some pertinent questions to ask:
1. Does your income depend on the money you receive from facilitating these meetings? Are you financially reliant on this income?
2. Do you view these meetings as a business model? Are you selling something to us? What are you selling, and do you have an interest in us returning to your meetings?
3. As a teacher, do you unintentionally create students who require instruction? What are you teaching them that they do not already know?
4. Do you engage in sexual relationships with students who depend on you?

Many spiritual teachers feed off the innocent ignorance and naivety of their students. Both parties perpetuate an unending cycle of co-dependency.

Illuminate the spiritual teacher-student relationship.

Most of us experience profound spiritual moments during 'spiritual meetings' and project these onto the teacher, who may even claim to be superior to their students. Such a teacher creates duality and suffering in their students.

**It's crucial to examine what differs in our inner dialogue during a spiritual meeting compared to our everyday, stressful, and fear-driven life patterns. What thoughts do we harbor, and how do they affect our breathing?
The higher our reverence for the teacher, the more we cultivate thoughts and corresponding emotions, projecting them onto the teacher. We begin to think that we are encountering God or the highest presence. As we innocently believe this, we feel safe, and our breathing patterns undergo a radical shift slowing down and deeper, allowing us to access our inner divine space.
This divine space must reside within us because we can feel it within ourselves, correct?
Once we discern our thoughts and feelings we create in a spiritual meeting, we can replicate them anywhere and at any time. By altering our breathing, turning our senses inward in meditation, or practicing Yoga or walking in nature, we can be truly free.**

If you chose to completely believe this realization, you are free! You can be in the presence of the highest divinity anytime, anywhere.

Yet, our old patterns of conditioned self-criticism ('I am never good enough') may resurface. We might believe that the outer teacher/master is more spiritually evolved than us and that we

need them (especially if the teacher continually emphasizes that your self is underdeveloped and incapable of judgment).
Now we must truly listen and fully comprehend: As long as we inhabit a human body on this planet, we will inevitably experience human emotions such as anger, hatred, pain, despair, drama, and sadness. And so it the teacher! We are connected to this world through resonance; you can simply open your eyes and observe your surroundings. If someone claims to be disconnected from this world and has achieved a special enlightened status, their authenticity is very questionable.

With this realization, we can deeply relax and embrace our human experience with love. We are all one and in the same boat. This human experience is simply as it is. We did not create this 'mess'; we were born into these bodies to gain ultimate wisdom.

You are entirely innocent and pure just as you are! Scientifically, there is evidence of a spiritual center in our brains (the Parietal Cortex), where spirituality resides. To access this, we enjoy going within, via deeper breathing, turning our senses inwards and enjoying a divine conversation inside.

Chapter 18

Kill the Buddha

If You Meet The Buddha On The Road, Kill Him?
BY CHRIS PACHECO

"As the psychotherapist and author Sheldon Kopp once said, "If you have a hero, look again: you have diminished yourself in some way." Kopp goes on to say, "The most important things that each man/woman must learn, no one else can teach him. Once he/she accepts this disappointment, he will be able to stop depending on the therapist, the guru who turns out to be just another struggling human being."

Rather than seeking a teacher to show me the way, I needed to become the way myself, through my own practice, through deep contemplation.

Idolizing a teacher is one side of the dilemma. The other lies in the teachings themselves. Over the life of our spiritual practice, there may be times when we begin to conceptualize the non-conceptual. We begin to "know" rather than remain open to. Killing the Buddha means killing our conceptualizations, killing the belief that we understand it all. This might seem counterintuitive; after all, if we let go of our knowledge, what's left? Total exposure. It consists of the openness of all experiences, the certainty of uncertainty, the security of insecurity, and the comfort in vulnerability. It's being courageously present, whatever that means, with things just as they are. We are each our own teacher and simultaneously each our own teaching.
It's at that point in we've come full circle.
When we kill the Buddha, we can transcend."

Chapter 19

Black vs. White Magic

Black vs. white magic:

Creating dependency vs. empowering freedom.

Abuse vs. support.

Fear-mongering vs. self-confidence.

Creating the feeling of unworthiness vs. supporting real power inside.

"You are never good enough" vs. "you are really good enough".

"You are worth nothing" vs. "You are worth everything".

Creating smallness vs. awakening divine greatness, bliss, and joy within.

"Your self is not capable" vs. "your self is super capable".

Foolishness vs. wisdom.

Childishness vs. adulthood.

Mistrust vs. trust.

Low energy vs. high energy.

Critique vs. pos. affirmation.

Self-centeredness vs. supportive light being.

Selling vs. sharing.

Manipulation vs. fulfillment.

Pressure vs. spaciousness.

Sexual power abuse vs. consensual love.

Secrets vs. openness.

Lies vs. honesty.

Brainwashing vs. empowering.

Sheep-status vs. realization

Taking vs. exchange.

Narcissist/superiority complex abusing inferiority complex vs. human being meeting human being in love.

Chapter 20

Spiritual Groups

Our life is centered around honest awareness!

Spiritual groups can initially help us experience our true nature as a flow of love, community, communion, and oneness. These transcendental experiences are felt inside and may be magnified by the presence of a spiritual group and teacher, which is a valuable and positive experience.

However, it's essential to move beyond our projections onto the group and teacher. Why?

Most of us are unaware of the unwritten and unseen rules in any religious or spiritual group. When we join a group, we unconsciously agree to these invisible rules. Depending on the group or cult, this may include signing up to perpetually be a student who will never attain bliss solely because of the group's structure. To illustrate, attending a Catholic church can expose us to the unspoken doctrines of guilt and original sin, implying that we are inherently sinners simply by being human. In some cases, informal group agreements may obligate us to unquestioningly obey a charismatic but potentially manipulative priest, teacher, or guru who could misuse power, seek money, or engage in unethical relationships.

Ultimately, true wisdom, peace, and love can only be found within ourselves, as it is our inherent birthright.

So, what can we do?

Enjoy the beauty and power of togetherness within your group.

Take the opportunity to learn and understand the informal laws and dynamics of your group.

Be prepared and feel the freedom to leave at any time, allowing yourself to fully embrace the inner light.

Indeed, leaving the comfort and togetherness of a spiritual group can come with its own set of challenges and adjustments. It's important for individuals to be aware of and prepared for these potential consequences.

Transform into a master of love rather than remaining a perpetual student.

Chapter 21

Reflections Concerning Partnership and Sexuality

Men and women, great opposites, great polarities, and great opportunities for love to triumph on all levels: spiritual, mental, and physical.

One of our strongest emotionally manifested beliefs and wishes is the profound longing we all share: to experience the complete and nourishing love and embrace from our mothers and fathers. The fact that our parents, due to their humanity, were unable to provide this complete love has resulted in one of the most significant traumas in all of us. It stands as our greatest source of emotional pain.

Consciously or unconsciously, we project this yearning for love onto our partners, hoping they will offer us unconditional, divine love and, in doing so, heal our deep-seated emotional wounds.

Recognizing this reality on our planet, men and women possess immense potential to learn to love each other without the burden of expectations and pressure.

We are all aware of the subtle yet profoundly important differences between men and women. These distinctions hold the power to help us understand, feel, and heal our relationships. The differences between the sexes can trigger old childhood wounds and trauma, providing an opportunity for our healing journey.

Every challenge, problem, and difficulty we encounter serves as an invitation for our true essence and the core of love within us to recognize and realize its innate spiritual nature: the ability to be pure love without expectations and physical needs.

This process may involve painful periods of unlearning deeply physically ingrained beliefs. These periods can be excruciating and isolating.

It is crucial to understand that our partners cannot provide us with perfect, complete divine love. They, too, are navigating the complexities of the human experience.

True divine love can only be found within ourselves. From that inner wellspring, we can share it with our partners.

Initially, we embark on our healing journey, and then we can support them with our love and clarity.

Tantric love, as one of the classic Indian paths to enlightenment, is a genuine and profound practice, much like the path of Yoga.

And ultimately, we are complete spiritual beings, free from the constraints of any particular path or needs.

Enlightenment is the process of wholeheartedly embracing the purest love within us, free from any sexual desires, attachments, or addictions. It signifies that we do not need therapy or healing at our core; we can seek assistance from others, but it is not a necessity.

The attachment to and compulsory engagement in sexual desires stand in contrast to the path towards the spiritual. One path leads to absolute freedom, while the other entraps us in the impermanent physical world.

Entering our reality of enlightenment also means entering the realm of the eternal orgasm, which transcends the physical. Everything we deeply desire and yearn for resides within us!

Chapter 22

You Are The Light of the World

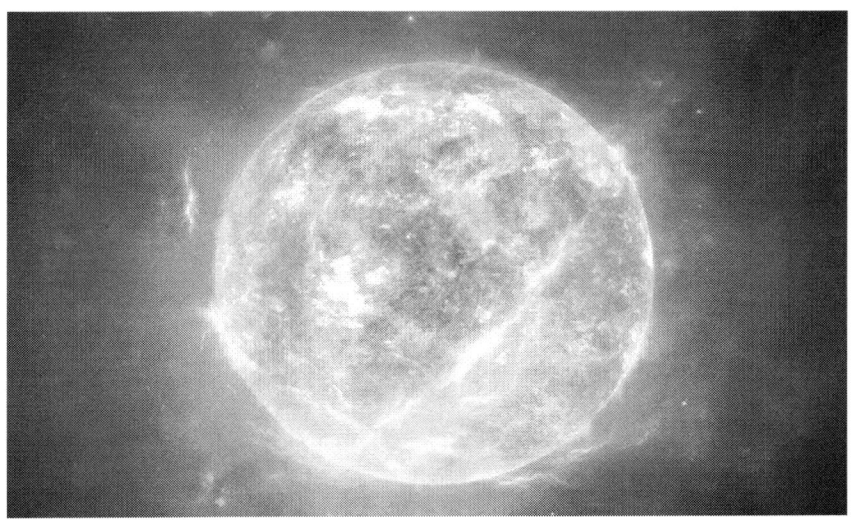

You are the light of the world!

You are the sunshine and source of happiness in your cosmos!

As I delve deeper into my divine being, I come to realize that I am the light of the world.

Now, we venture into the realm of the mystical: Every individual is the sole light in the universe!

There exists no valid external source of happiness outside of oneself. No partner, family member, friend, or material possession can serve as a true source of happiness in the grand tapestry of existence with GOD.

It is a common temptation for us humans to project our happiness onto the material world, which includes our relationships with other human beings. While we are deeply interconnected, it's akin to our profound identification with our own physical bodies.

Our wise Indian friends affirm that it is but Māyā, our entanglement in the material world of myriad distractions, that obstructs our path to enlightenment.

Let me pose these fundamental questions:
- Where does our body and our world go when we drift into slumber?
- What unfolds when we follow our breath, slipping into the space between inhaling and exhaling?
- Where do we, as beings, venture when our physical bodies transform into dust?

You are the solitary fount of genuine happiness and light in your Cosmos.

God, is simply the experience of the most exquisite love and light that resides within you. It can only be found within your brain, as the complete story of our lives unfolds there and nowhere else.

No more teacher, no more student. In this realization, the concept of a teacher and student becomes inherently dishonest, for there is only the warm, relaxing light within. It's akin to diving and swimming into the source of an ocean of tender, loving warmth.

Come and immerse yourself in the profound peace of ultimate fulfillment.

Your spiritual empowerment resides as the highest energy, as God within you. Once you've experienced unconditional love, it becomes a well-established place in your brain that you can access at any time by simply engaging in a loving conversation within yourself.

Anyone who suggests that your self is anything less than a manifestation of complete love is resonating with our 'guilt-self,' which is riddled with fear, shame, and an inferiority complex, all in an attempt to manipulate you. You need not be a puppet in this game. The moment you sense this resonance, return swiftly to the all-encompassing divine love within.

You are perfect, complete love within.

We can deeply love ourselves as the perfect, understanding parent we longed for in our youth.

No more guilt, no more shame, no more projections—only warm, enveloping love.
Embrace it and enjoy.

Chapter 23

Ask And You Will Receive

On one level of our existence, we humans are remarkably powerful beings capable of co-creating our universe. Choices like pursuing a degree, starting a business, maintaining a marriage, or ending it are decisions we can make and, with determination, often achieve our worldly objectives.

In addition to this worldly power, we all possess a similar magical power of creation on the spiritual plane of our existence. This spiritual power allows us to connect with and manifest higher states of consciousness, love, and bliss within ourselves, transcending the limitations of our everyday human experience.

When we open ourselves to the incredible possibility of attaining complete enlightenment and ask for it persistently, we can receive what we seek. This acknowledgment underscores the profound influence our intentions and beliefs can have on our spiritual journey.

When you open up to the unbelievable possibility of receiving complete enlightenment, if you ask with persistence, you will receive what you are asking for.

Chapter 24

You are the Master

Nobody has more wisdom than you.

Nobody has more love than you.

Nobody "knows" more than you do.

Nobody has realized more than you.

Nobody has power over you.

Nobody has more bliss than you.

If anybody claims that they do, he/she is lying and is likely attempting to manipulate or deceive you.

If we feel any lacking inside, we need to really look into our created belief system: where/how do I outsource my love?

Self-inquiry is simply: Who/what am I really? Thoughts, feelings, and bodies come and go. There is always something eternal and blissful inside.

Following our breath is always available as long this body is alive.

EMDR/bilateral stimulation can heal any trauma in our brain.

Chapter 25

What is Breathing your Body?

Who is breathing your body?

What is breathing your body?

The answer is absolute freedom now and here.

Chapter 26

Real Joy

I love to let go of all ideas about my life.

I love to let go of the idea of my life.

I love to let go of my life.

Chapter 27

Your Book of Love

The reality of your enlightenment.

Truly embracing this possibility for your life could lead us into a state of complete and utter relaxation and bliss.

The book of your life is already written:

There is no choice, there is no coincidence; there is only the journey from love and back to love, all unfolding within the realm of love.

One of the most pervasive illusions we humans entertain is the illusion of choice. It gives rise to an unending fear of making wrong decisions, which in turn can create pain and suffering into our lives.

You might ponder, 'But I worked so hard to make my relationship or my business work,' or 'I choose between ordering a latte or tea every day.' These choices may seem very real on a surface level.

Now, here are some thought-provoking questions:

- Do you genuinely believe you chose the way your body looked when you were born?

- Do you truly think you chose your current physical appearance?

- Did you consciously select your parents and siblings?

- Were you the architect of the country you were born in?

- Did you design the environment, nature, and society you were born into?

- Did you orchestrate the 'coincidences' that led you to find your partner, friends, and more?

- Did you personally dictate how the trillions of cells and atoms comprising your brain and body function?

- Can you honestly claim to have chosen all of your thoughts and feelings?

In all honesty, on a limited scale of existence, it might appear that we have choices. However, when we consider the grander and more profound perspective, it seems that much of it is predetermined...

We may appear to have choices on various levels. Yet, it's possible that there exists a pre-written script of our lives, and we are often under the influence of illusions about it.

The Indian sage Papaji once declared, 'Nothing ever happened!' Why? Because our seemingly stable universe is, in reality, quite unstable. It's composed of fluctuating particles that exist in different locations simultaneously. Moreover, these particles exhibit characteristics of both waves and particles at the same time. Quantum physicists will affirm that the essence of our cosmos remains elusive, and nothing is definitively real—almost like being able to move your hand through your body.

According to brain research, the entire movie of your life is created within your brain, and your five senses merely serve to confirm the narrative. This scenario sounds a little bit similar to concepts of the movie "The Matrix".

Also, contemplating the billions of galaxies and solar systems akin to ours, can we genuinely assume that our 'decisions' hold central significance in the cosmos?

Imagine if we could fully relax into accepting the book of life as it is. Picture all the stress associated with making the best decisions and avoiding poor choices dissipating.

In my view, at a profoundly deep level of existence, the book is already written. When I acknowledge my 'thrownness' into life (a term coined by the German philosopher Martin Heidegger), there is an exquisite sense of relief and relaxation.

For me, we are all, on a superficial level, seemingly on a journey (which is evidently scripted in your book of life) :-)

In the journey to and from love, in every single moment, we have the opportunity to immerse ourselves in the love from which we originate and into which we will eventually return.

In this perspective, the book of life transforms into your book of love!

Chapter 28

Spiritual Practice

"In our divine core, there is no space, no time, no path, and certainly no need for spiritual practice. That is the realm of our divine love, light, and bliss—a state of existence beyond practice."

Also, there's the human level of existence within a physical body, complete with all its challenges in space and time. Our enlightenment involves embracing and loving our human experience—seeing it, embracing it, and loving it. This, in essence, is our spiritual practice.

Whatever method you've found to open your heart and connect with your divine self—whether it's through meditation, Yoga, dancing, or communing with nature—it's all valid.

NO, NO, NO to discipline.

Why? Because it's a love relationship between your divine core and yourself, a connection and merging with your core. Love doesn't require discipline. It's like having a dear friend you're so deeply in love with that you're naturally and eagerly excited to meet them. No discipline needed, right?

Some days, I find it lovely to rise at 4:00 or 5:00 in the morning and spend 1, 2, or 3 hours delving into the Divine within. But there's no 'must,' and there's no set schedule; it's more of an organic flow. Some days, it happens early in the morning, and other days, it doesn't.

Once again, I don't recommend using force or discipline. The more you push with willpower in one direction, the more resistance you may encounter. Spirituality thrives in subtlety and love.

Our spiritual experiences often come in waves. Some weeks, we may experience profound entry into blissful dimensions, while in other weeks, not much may occur, or we may confront challenging emotions.

Mornings are a wonderful time for meditation. I also recommend evenings before bedtime. Mornings provide an excellent opportunity to ease into the bliss of existence because the energy of the night is still present. Nighttime energy contains an element of 'letting go', a little dying, as we release our daily lives to fall asleep. Meditating before sleep is highly recommended as it allows us to let go and 'complete' the day's experiences, surrendering to the highest.

Mindfulness and Enlightenment

In starting my spiritual practice, I always make it a point to see, acknowledge, and embrace all the energies and emotions within.

> The most crucial aspect is creating a loving inner dialogue: acknowledging and embracing everything happening within. I learn to hold myself warmly amidst desperation, hatred, anger, envy, pain, drama, and whatever else I notice inside. This inner dialogue is a form of self-love therapy that we can practice. If we find certain feelings too intense to embrace, it's perfectly okay to seek assistance from a therapist to learn how to embrace ourselves.
>
> It is our divine mind: Use it creatively! It is your friend helping you to enter and enjoy the highest bliss in the universe via

creating a most beautiful and loving inner conversation expressing thoughts of the highest vibration. Harness the power of your divine mind to guide your thoughts and intentions toward the highest states of consciousness, love, and bliss. This inner conversation with yourself, filled with thoughts of the highest vibration, will lead you to a profound and transformative experience of the divine within.

Deep breathing is of utmost importance. Breath is a close companion to our life energy, and the deeper we breathe, the more life energy we can infuse into our bodies. Ancient Indian sages recommend exploring the space between inhaling and exhaling. If you wish, you can create a gentle pause between the inhale and exhale.

I also always recommend using headphones and listening to nature sounds or spiritual sacred music, such as Tibetan chants, for bilateral stimulation.

Within your core awaits only nourishing love, light, and bliss—as you. That is who we are. Enjoy being the core and source of bliss, love, and light in your life!"

[2] https://around.uoregon.edu/content/neuroscientist-talk-about-how-brain-creates-reality

[3] https://www.npr.org/transcripts/654730916

[4] elements - Science Education at Jefferson Lab." https://education.jlab.org/qa/atomicstructure_11.html.

[5] Facts About Hydrogen | Live Science." 23 Jan. 2015, https://www.livescience.com/28466-hydrogen.html.

[6] 99.9999999% of Your Body Is Empty Space - ScienceAlert." 23 Sep. 2016, https://www.sciencealert.com/99-9999999-of-your-body-is-empty-space.

[7] Robert Coolman | Live Science - https://www.livescience.com/author/robert-coolman

Manufactured by Amazon.ca
Bolton, ON